SPACE DISCOVERIES

by TAMRA B. ORR

Raintree is an imprint of Capstone Global Library Limited, a company incorporated in England and Wales having its registered office at 264 Banbury Road, Oxford, OX2 7DY – Registered company number: 6695582

www.raintree.co.uk
myorders@raintree.co.uk

Edited by Michelle Hasselius
Designed by Heidi Thompson
Original illustrations © Capstone Global Library Limited 2019
Picture research by Svetlana Zhurkin
Production by Kris Wilfahrt
Originated by Capstone Global Library Ltd
Printed and bound in India

ISBN 978 1 4747 5969 4 (hardback)
22 21 20 19 18
10 9 8 7 6 5 4 3 2 1

ISBN 978 1 4747 5973 1 (paperback)
23 22 21 20 19
10 9 8 7 6 5 4 3 2 1

British Library Cataloguing in Publication Data
A full catalogue record for this book is available from the British Library.

Our very special thanks to Valerie Neal, Chair, Space History Department at the National Air and Space Museum, for her review. Capstone would also like to thank the following at Smithsonian Enterprises: Kealy Gordon, Product Development Manager; Ellen Nanney, Licensing Manager; Brigid Ferraro, Vice President, Education and Consumer Products; and Carol LeBlanc, Senior Vice President, Education and Consumer Products.

Acknowledgements
We would like to thank the following for permission to reproduce photographs: AP Images: Neal Hamberg, 28 (left); B. Saxton/NRAO/AUI/NSF, 28 (right); ESO: L. Calçada/M. Kornmesser, 21 (back); NASA: 12, 17 (inset), 19, 23, 27, Ames/JPL-Caltech, 24-25, Ames/JPL-Caltech/T. Pyle, 26, Charles Babir, 16 (right), Chris Gunn, 13, Dana Berry/Sky Works Digital, 21 (inset), ESA/A. Feild (STScI), 9, ESA/H. Bond (STScI)/M. Barstow (University of Leicester), 29, Goddard Space Flight Center/CI Lab, 20, Goddard/Arizona State University, 22 (top), JPL, cover (bottom), 10, JPL/Space Science Institute, 4, JPL/USGS, 8, JPL-Caltech, 6, 11, Ken Ulbrich, 18, SDO, 17 (back); Newscom: Zuma Press/Mainichi Newspaper, 15; Shutterstock: Guilherme Mesquita, 5, Kathy Hutchins, 16 (left), Radoslaw Lecyk, 22 (bottom), Rosamund Parkinson, 7, seecreateimages, cover (background), Vadim Sadovski, 14

Quote Sources
Page 7, "Small Asteroid Is Earth's Constant Companion." 15 June 2016. NASA. https://www.nasa.gov/feature/jpl/small-asteroid-is-earths-constant-companion

Page 13, "Hubble Reveals Observable Universe Contains 10 Times More Galaxies Than Previously Thought." 13 October 2016. NASA. https://www.nasa.gov/feature/goddard/2016/hubble-reveals-observable-universe-contains-10-times-more-galaxies-than-previously-thought

CONTENTS

ENDLESS EXPLORATION

Have you ever looked up at the night sky and wondered what is out there? What hasn't been discovered yet – new planets, more galaxies, little green men?

Since the first telescope was invented more than 400 years ago, people have been looking up to the sky. The drive to find out what is out there has grown since then. In the 1960s, the United States began sending spaceships and astronauts to the Moon. Since then space missions and space probes have discovered moons, planets and stars that we didn't know existed before. What else is still up there waiting to be discovered?

MORE MOONS

EARTH'S MINI MOON?

Earth is being followed – by a mini moon. In 2016, NASA
scientists spotted a large asteroid circling Earth. The asteroid
was named 2016 H03. It is 37 to 91 metres (120 to 300 feet) wide.
Nicknamed the mini moon, the asteroid moves around our planet
like a satellite. Both the asteroid and Earth orbit the Sun together.

The 2016 H03 asteroid is also called a near–Earth companion.

Sun ▶ ·

Earth ▶

◀2016 HO3

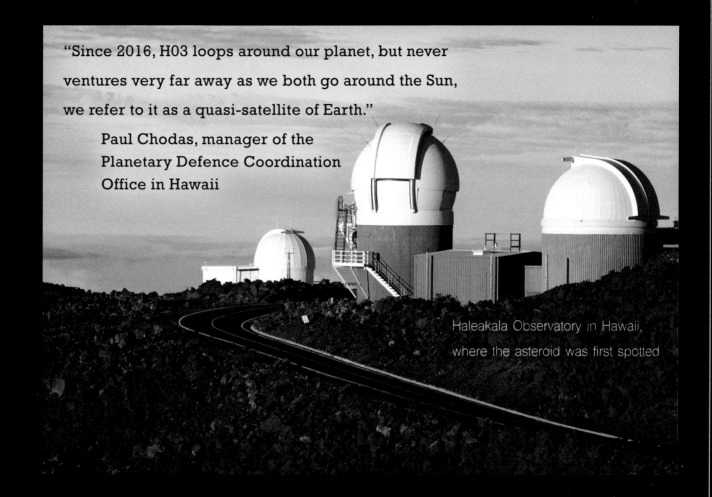

"Since 2016, H03 loops around our planet, but never ventures very far away as we both go around the Sun, we refer to it as a quasi-satellite of Earth."

Paul Chodas, manager of the Planetary Defence Coordination Office in Hawaii

Haleakala Observatory in Hawaii, where the asteroid was first spotted

The newly discovered asteroid might be NASA's next space mission. Scientists believe a space probe could reach the asteroid in about 65 days.

A MOON FOR NEPTUNE

In 2013, scientists discovered that the planet Neptune has another moon. The new moon is called S/2004 N1. It is 20 kilometres (12.5 miles) wide. Scientist Mark Showalter was looking through some photographs taken by the Hubble Space Telescope. The Hubble uses a digital camera to take detailed photos of the universe. Showalter saw an unexpected dot in these photos. That dot turned out to be S/2004 N1. Scientists plan to give S/2004 N1 a new name in the future. For now, most experts refer to it as "that little moon".

▼Neptune   ▲ Triton

Triton is Neptune's largest moon.
It is 2,700 km (1,680 miles) wide.

Proteus

Naiad

Galatea

Thalassa

Neptune

Despina

Larissa

Newly discovered moon
(S/2004 N1)

Neptune is the fourth largest
planet in our solar system.
It has more than 12 moons.

JUPITER AND JUNO

On 5 August 2011, the *Juno* space probe was launched to study the planet Jupiter. The unmanned spacecraft entered Jupiter's orbit on 4 July 2016. Since then, *Juno* has circled the planet several times. It has recorded new information about Jupiter's size, temperature and weather. The space probe has also taken stunning photos. Scientists were surprised by Jupiter's bright colours. *Juno* will remain in space until at least July 2018.

The *Juno* space probe cost more than $1 billion to build. It travels at speeds of 265,059 km (164,700 miles) per hour.

◄ Juno

Juno is not the first space probe to study Jupiter. NASA's *Pioneer* and *Voyager* probes flew by the planet in the 1970s. They took basic photos and measurements of Jupiter.

CASSINI'S DISCOVERIES

In 1997 NASA launched the *Cassini* space probe to study Saturn.

launched	1997
first mission completed	June 2008 (mission extended to September 2010)
travelled	7.8 billion kilometres (4.9 billion miles)
collected	635 gigabytes of data
captured	more than 453,000 photographs
discovered	6 moons, 3 seas and 2 oceans
orbited Saturn	294 times

In 2016, astronomers were shocked to discover that the universe is much bigger than they thought. At first, scientists thought there were 200 billion galaxies in space. Now astronomers believe the universe has 2 trillion galaxies!

This discovery is based on photographs from the Hubble Space Telescope. Astronomers were able to create a 3D map of the universe based on this new data.

Hubble Space Telescope

"It boggles the mind that over 90 per cent of the galaxies in the universe have yet to be studied. Who knows what interesting properties we will find when we observe these galaxies with the next generation of telescopes?"

Christopher Conselice, astrophysicist

The new James Webb Space Telescope will be able to look further into space than any other telescope ever used.

Today the planet Mars is frozen and dry. But NASA researchers have found that this may not always have been the case. In 2017, researchers discovered that a massive asteroid crashed into Mars about 3 billion years ago. It landed in one of the planet's largest oceans. The asteroid created mega tsunamis all over Mars. The push and pull of water from the tsunamis left a large crater on the planet's surface. Scientists believe this crater will prove that Mars once had lakes, rivers, seas and oceans – just like Earth. That means it might have had life on it too.

Researchers believe that the tsunami waves on Mars were almost 152 metres (500 feet) tall. In 2011, the tsunami waves that crashed into Japan were 39 m (128 feet) tall. The 2004 tsunami in Indonesia had waves 30.5 m (100 feet) tall.

the 2011 tsunami in Miyagi, Japan

THE SPACE TRAVEL BUSINESS

Launching a rocket into space is exciting – and expensive. And rockets can only be used once. But this is changing. Private companies, such as SpaceX, have found ways to build recyclable rockets. These rockets have been designed to return to Earth and be used again. So far SpaceX has sent these rockets to the International Space Station (ISS) and back. Currently the company is trying to send a crew of astronauts into space. To do this they will use their *Dragon* spacecraft, a rocket that can fit up to seven people inside. The company hopes to send astronauts to Mars one day.

Elon Musk founded SpaceX. In the *Iron Man* films, Robert Downey Jr. based his portrayal of Tony Stark on Musk.

SPACEX'S DSCOVR SATELLITE

In 2015, SpaceX partnered with the US Air Force and NASA to launch a satellite into deep space. The DSCOVR satellite was built to keep a close eye on the Sun's solar flares. Solar flares are sudden bursts of radiation from the Sun's surface. These flares can affect radios, power lines and mobile phones on Earth. The DSCOVR satellite sends a warning to scientists around the world if a flare is detected.

In Florida, USA, scientists get the DSCOVR satellite ready to launch.

SpaceX is not the only private company in the space travel business. A number of other companies are queuing up for the chance to launch rockets into space. Large companies such as Boeing and Lockheed Martin usually build military planes and passenger aircraft. Now they are building spacecraft to take astronauts and special equipment to the ISS.

The Sierra Nevada Corporation has created a mini space shuttle called the Dream Chaser. The Dream Chaser can carry two to seven people. It is scheduled to start sending supplies to the ISS around 2020.

Lockheed Martin's *Orion* ground test vehicle arrived at the Kennedy Space Center on 21 April 2012.

GOLDEN SKIES

On 17 August 2017, there was a huge explosion in space. Two stars crashed into each other, filling the universe with gold, silver and platinum. The event is known as a kilonova. You couldn't see it in the sky, but astronomers were watching. Back on Earth, satellite and telescope sensors went off across the world. For the first time in history, scientists had the technology to know where to look to see this rare event.

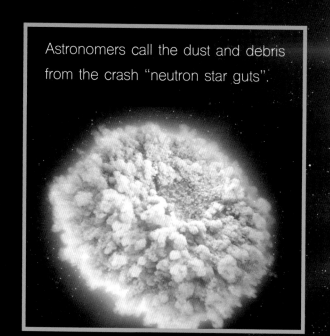

Astronomers call the dust and debris from the crash "neutron star guts".

Experts believe the two stars were swirling around each other at one thousand times per second before they crashed into each other.

HOME, SWEET LAVA TUBE

In October 2017 researchers from Japan spotted a giant hole in the Moon. The hole leads down to a long, hollow lava tube. The tube is huge. Scientists believe it could hold a city as big as Philadelphia, USA, inside.

The Earth also has lava tubes. But none of them are close to the size of the one found on the Moon.

Thurston lava tube in Hawaii

A lava tube is formed when lava flows under the ground. The outside of the tube crusts over. Astronauts could use lava tubes to protect themselves from meteor storms and extreme temperatures on the Moon. Perhaps one day, these tubes could even be used to create the first human civilization on the Moon. People could live on the Moon for weeks or longer.

Astronauts cannot survive for more than three days on the Moon. Their spacesuits are not designed to be on the Moon for long periods of time.

Astronaut Eugene A. Cernan drove the Lunar Roving Vehicle on the Moon in December 1972.

KEPLER 10c

Look at that! It's Godzilla! No, we're not talking about the fictional monster. Godzilla is a giant planet. Using the Kepler Space Telescope, astronomers discovered the planet in May 2011. It's called Kepler 10c. It's 560 light years away from Earth. The planet is 17 times heavier than Earth and twice the size. Scientists believe it is 11 billion years old.

Scientists also call the planet mega-Earth.

Kepler 10c

Kepler 10c takes 45 days to circle around its sun-like star. Earth takes 365 days to circle around our Sun.

KEPLER 37B

Finding the planet Kepler 37b was a challenge for scientists. It is only about one-third the size of Earth. That's even smaller than Mercury, the smallest planet in our solar system. NASA scientists found the planet in February 2013. It is located about 210 light years away from Earth.

Kepler 37b may be little, but it is hot. Scientists believe that the planet's average temperature is about 426 degrees Celsius (800 degrees Fahrenheit). That is hot enough to melt the zinc inside a penny!

THE KEPLER SPACE TELESCOPE

One of the reasons that the world knows so much about space is because of space telescopes such as the Hubble Space Telescope and the Kepler Space Telescope. These telescopes are like floating science labs, equipped with recorders, cameras and computer chips. All of the information they gather is sent back to Earth for scientists to study.

The Kepler Space Telescope was launched into space in 2009. It has 42 cameras. The telescope is pointed at a single spot in the sky. Built-in sensors watch the spot carefully. The Kepler Space Telescope has found more than 4,000 planets so far.

THE DIAMOND STAR

Imagine a diamond the size of Earth. It would have trillions of trillions of carats. Astronomers spotted a diamond this size in 2014. Named PSR J2222-0137, the diamond is about 11 billion years old. It is 900 light years away from Earth.

The largest diamond on Earth is the Golden Jubilee. It has 546 carats. The large diamond was found in South Africa.

A white dwarf star and PSR J2222-0137 orbit around each other.

This diamond is formed from a white dwarf star. After a star ages and dies, it turns into a white dwarf star. Over billions of years, the dwarf star crystallizes. It gets smaller, colder and dimmer. The inside of the white dwarf star turns into a diamond.

white dwarf star called Sirius B

Scientists believe that our Sun will become a white dwarf star in 5 billion years. About 2 billion years after that, it will crystallize. Then the Sun will become a giant diamond in the centre of our solar system.

GLOSSARY

asteroid large rock that travels through space

astronaut person who is trained to live and work in space

astronomer scientist who studies stars, planets and other objects in space

carat unit for measuring the weight of precious gems and metals

crater hole made when large pieces of rock crash into a planet's or moon's surface

crystallize form crystals

galaxy large group of stars and planets

gigabyte unit used to measure the amount of data storage; a gigabyte is 1 billion bytes

light year unit for measuring distance in space

meteor chunk of metal or stone that falls from space; a meteor is also called a shooting star

NASA US government agency that researches flight and space exploration

orbit path an object follows as it goes around a sun or a planet

platinum valuable silver-white metal that is often used in jewellery

satellite object that moves around Earth in space, communicating or collecting information

solar system a sun and all the planets, moons and smaller objects moving around it

space probe spacecraft without a crew that is used to explore space

tsunami very large wave

COMPREHENSION AND RESEARCH QUESTIONS

1. Describe what happens during a kilonova.

2. Using the Kepler Space Telescope, scientists have discovered the planets Kepler 10c and Kepler 37b. Name another planet that scientists have found with this telescope. Write about some of the planet's interesting features.

3. In your own words, describe how a diamond is formed in space.

FIND OUT MORE

BOOKS

Incredible Robots in Space (Incredible Robots), Louise and Richard Spilsbury (Raintree, 2018)

Knowledge Encyclopedia Space!: The Universe as You've Never Seen it Before, DK (DK Children, 2015)

The Sun and Our Solar System (Great Scientific Theories), Jen Green (Raintree, 2017)

WEBSITES

Find out more about the Hubble Space Telescope at: **www.dkfindout.com/uk/explore/all-about-hubble-space-telescope**

Learn more about our universe and space exploration at: **www.esa.int/esaKIDSen**

INDEX